moon full of moons

moon full of moons

poetry of transformation

To Kim + Moose glow from within ✱D

Kat Lehmann

PEACEFUL DAILY, INC.

Kat Lehmann

Library of Congress Control Number: 2014955136

Published by Peaceful Daily, Inc.
www.peacefuldaily.com

ISBN 978-0-9884926-4-6
EISBN 978-0-9884926-5-3

Book design by Perseus-Design.com
Printed in the United States of America.
First Edition

10 9 8 7 6 5 4 3 2 1

Dedicated to my family, my friends,
and my friends who are family.

In particular, this book is dedicated to Ken, Sol, and Violet,
who give my heart imagination
and continue to grow with me each day in fullness.

Special thanks to Ken and Subha
who provided early comments and encouragement
as the circle of the Moon first took form.

Table of Contents

This fire-splattered night
will mirror the Sun
bit by bit
she circles around
her phases, she finds them
reflected within –
the Moon Full of Moons
has found fullness
again

Introduction / Interwoven

At times it can feel as if the beautiful ground is crumbling beneath our feet. During these sorrowful times, we may be inspired to build a bridge of hope and faith, and journey to an unknown land. This is a familiar story: the fall from a simple happiness through a time of struggle, to ultimately realize a more complicated happiness that is hard-won.

This transformation is mirrored in Nature, where all of us are interrelated and interwoven. If you look deeply at a river, a tree, the Moon, or yourself, eventually you will see pieces of everything else within it. In these pages, the Moon is our shining metaphor in the sky, a symbol for loss in the darkness that travels the arc from ruin to renewal and eventually realizes the light of a new happiness. The phases of the Moon are the phases of ourselves.

We begin with the **First Full Moon** ○, which describes a carefree innocence and an easy happiness, like that often associated with childhood. As the light dims – **Waning Gibbous** ◑, **Waning Half-Moon** ◐, **Waning Crescent** ● – feelings of melancholy, isolation, and hopelessness encroach. It may become a challenge to remember the possibility of happiness. We wane like the Moon.

In the midst of our darkest moments, we reach the **New Moon** ●. Be encouraged that we are not left in the deepest valley. Rather, we find the beginning of a new cycle. In the absence of the light, our eyes can adjust to the clarity of a new perspective. Simplify and purge the unnecessary and unhealthy things. Resolve to begin again.

When we find the strength to set down the weight we have been carrying, we can work toward a new cycle of wellness, reaching my favorite phase: **Waxing Crescent** ●. There will always be sad things, many of which are beyond our control. Waxing Crescent is the decision to take the first hopeful step across the bridge to a new place. Happiness may ask us to reinvent our lives along the way, but, *even from the wild fires, a new forest comes.*

As we "*pull down the Sun and glow from within*" and nurture good seeds as we find them – **Waxing Half-Moon ☽, Waxing Gibbous ☽** – the stamina involved in achieving happiness becomes evident. Even so, someone must live the story of overcoming great challenges. *Be like a tree that remains after the forest is cleared.*

We end with the **Second Full Moon ○**, which represents a perhaps more mature happiness: one that has experienced deep sadness but is determined to be happy, regardless. We are, again, open to the peaceful, the positive, and the beautiful. *There are small reminders of happiness scattered everywhere, like dandelions waiting to be seen as flowers.* Exercise happiness like a muscle, and, with time, happiness will grow stronger, like the light of the Moon.

There is a tendency to search for happiness outside ourselves until we realize that the capacity for happiness originates within us. And that's when we find it. *The mind guesses at what the heart already knows.*

Happiness is an ongoing process, one that perhaps is never finished. I forgive myself for the times I fall short. Respect your path, and consider that being a little damaged helps us to be there more fully for others.

"Don't work too hard,"
the river said,
"Some of this is downhill,
and the wandering
is the best part."

Nights of the First Full Moon

The sand of stars has grown a pearl —
of spiraled night and oceaned ear

A sea so deep has washed ashore
these songs that only I can hear

○

My grandmother's moon
was not a face of shadows
but a silhouette:

A young couple dancing
her long hair flowing
in the spin

Being a Poem

I opened a poem – crawled inside,
felt its rough edges around smooth, concave walls.
I – the little spoon – curled knees to chin and speechless
in the warmth as I dreamed.
Cautiously, I crept out (time later)
and steadied myself on the Moon.
The poem still flowed through me like blood
as if I had been born from it.
Its rhythm in my veins brought a spark
to my eyes and a sway
to my hips –
The poem was everywhere I looked.
It was grass bending in a breeze
that traveled the world,
reaching with fingers of wind
to gently slip over its green length
from broad base to icicle point.
The poem was breath
as my lungs expanded like inverted trees
transforming atmosphere and lightly releasing it
like a song.
I touched myself as if touching the poem
with the mastery of self-recognition
only to realize that
I am a poem
that stirs the souls of the lost and found
before sailing like a wisp
of one who cannot be owned
only borrowed.

Childhood Memories

The distance
of childhood memories
vague as glimpses
treefrogs and fireflies
crayfish river
swinging feet pointing
to the sky to hover
flip-flops sailing
riding the waves
a new friend to keep
canoe on the lake
oars long and deep
(algae clinging)
rocking and splashing
building a fort
a rabbit how close
the day sticky-hot
run under the hose
a bath with bubbles
and try not to sleep
animals to snuggle
blankets tucked tight
a wooden squirrel
and radio raccoon
wishing the twinkle
and the Moon
eyelids heavy, dreams take flight
I catch a falling star tonight

He is a Pond

for Sol

He is a pond

Ripples from the day subside
until he is
stillness
beneath the stars

The frogs of him
jumped
and rested

The Butterfly of Her Mind

for Violet

Somewhere in the darkness
her sigh
becomes audible, her
exhalations pronounced –
That's when
her wings stretch beyond
the confines of a day
and in that moment she is
found and free –
Soaring the butterfly
of her mind

I Want to Be Like a Tree

I want to be like a tree.

I want to give back to the Earth what I have borrowed,
nourish those who need it,
perform magical feats as I turn a star's gift into nectar.

I want to color the hillside and then let the color go,
freshen the air,
warm the cold night,

and maybe in a small way I will expand
the beauty of the world.

Peach

Eating a peach
demands one's full attention.
The world fades in the animalistic
sweet dripping
down to the stone.
Take my advice, it's best
to be prepared. Will it be
Napkin?
Sink?
The grass outside?
One thing is certain –
It is impossible to do anything else at the same time.
A peach is always eaten on its own terms.

Alive

This is where I am.
Soft breeze brushing bare skin,
a steady pull holding me to this spinning roundness,
chirps and rustles,
steam rising from my bowl, warmth of noodles,
a distant, airless fire
obscuring the infinite with blue-ceiling sky,
and animals of clouds drifting on the riverwind.

In this warm brightness of a day
I walk through the stiff reachings of green.
I am fully present.
Here. This moment.

And the moment is mine to have.

I have no need for anything
but the stirring air
and the slow jump-rope of the Sun
swinging around, shifting shadows.

I take in the air and release it
altered
as proof of my presence.

I am a part of this moment,
essential to its balance –
complete and interwoven.

This is the moment when I am alive.

Night of the Backwards Moon

Oh, the days
that we played
in the midnight sun —
our rivers ran up
as the two of us one.

Our fishes
were wishes
the stars would fall soon
as we dreamed the bright night
by a backwards moon.

Sleeping Colors

The colors are wrapped in blankets of grey –
they've tucked themselves in for the night.
They're dreaming of sunsets and prism bouquets
and snoozing 'til Sun's early rise.

They open their eyes to brighten the day –
mix pigments to threshold of white.
They're painting the world with their rainbows as they
ride morningbeams down from the skies.

Nights of Waning Gibbous

This fractured night
disintegrates
in borrowed light –
its circle scattered
by dark breath
the star-seeds of
a dandelion spent

☽

The Moon runs laps like a curator
inspecting her greatest prize

The path she clears is hers alone
as she reigns uncertain skies

Measuring Life

A honeybee lives for weeks
but her life's sweet work survives for decades.

Trees appear to be born each spring
but their rings tell a different story.

Oceans feel ageless.
Their time is measured in the breadth of their beaches.

Stars seem eternal,
but their lifetime is measured in the composition of their cores.

Is a person's life measured
in years, or

how they reinvented themselves in change of season –
like a tree,

by the breadth of their work –
like an ocean,

by the composition of their core –
like a star,

and by what they leave behind –
like a bee?

The Baby That Time Grew Up

It's the same child, I think.
Cheekbones, eyes, hair, the same.
I hold the hand that exerts your will,
much bigger now,
my favorite crease of your palm
flattened
by the growth of years.
Your precious foot
that fit in the palm of my hand
now carries you down the hill at full speed.
My baby is here yet my baby is gone,
a certain sadness.
You no longer fit across my lap.
You are too big to climb
Mommy Mountain.
You don't remember any of it.
The long nights pacing. How I nursed you
every few hours for months.
How I loved your baby-seriousness.
How we loved exploring. How we loved.
We took long walks,
I wore you in front and
you held my finger and steered
which way to go.
We turned corners together, tethered as one.
Now you run ahead, so big,
my baby deep in your archeology.
Only I remember.
But maybe somewhere inside, you remember too.
Like a cloud with an indescribable shape,
or rushing riverwater that is forever blurry.
Relics of how we loved.
How we still do.

Solomon Sleeps

He is tired,
like an imploding star. He releases his last energy going supernova.

We snuggle under blankets with stuffed animals.
Reading and giggling, listening
to night-sounds
like a slumber party.

I hold him close, his small body
succumbs to sleep with a slight twitch
as his breath deepens.
It's the best part of my day.

I feel the flutter of my fingertip-pulse
against the undulations of his breathing.

We are different tempos now,
like syncopation of an erratic jazz.
I press my ear to his chest to hear
his secret drumbeat.

We were one rhythm once,
now we are two.

Seven Violet Nights

1

Now night has fallen, the stars shining high
Dreamland is calling for my girl and I.
She glows like a miracle moon in my sky
Ruling the room with soft, cinnamon eyes.

2

The day melts away as she melts in my arms.
Just flow like a river to sleep, Little One.
Her chin tips back slightly, her body serene –
Let go and breathe sweetly, now drift into dreams.

3

Her rhythm of breathing is waves like the sea.
She wraps snug around me, her island to be.
She warms my wide beaches, laps long, rocky shores,
Erodes my rough edges, together once more.

4

Rocking in rhythm (our bedtime routine) –
Hearts puffed to soaring, her breathing, the breeze.
Eyes closed in dreaming, wrapped up soft and warm –
Our night's destination: the bright morning shores.

5

Our bodies in balance, a union of two –
Our own ecosystem, our planet so new.
Bound in connectedness, sameness of essence:
Present and future, two women connected.

6

A magical being, so perfect, so warm –
She sinks into snuggles, falls limp in my arms.
Raptured, entranced in her bright starlit charms,
I'll hold her all night 'til she wakes with the dawn.

7

Under the infinite, wrapped in the night:
Our two generations, woven by fate.
Asleep and secure, two lives find their rhyme –
She knows I will care for her…'til it's her time

Life as a Shadow

Turn off the light to get rid of a shadow.
Turn on the light to liberate it.

I wish I could sink into shadow – and swim –
With the things the day left behind.
We shadows, we'd pool together (black ooze)
And paint a splendid new night.
Connected in airless floating we'd watch
The Sun dip itself into night-dye,

Like raindrops that dive in the ocean and swim
And bathe in the darkness so free.
Each morning, we'd disassemble and fly
Like new blackbirds that lift up the day,
And sail flatly across the not-sky to find
A bright wisdom with every dawn.

Perspective

From across the Milky Way,
Sol is a distant star,
part of a constellation
embodying an alien mythology.

The universe looks different
from there, an unknown outpost
surrounded by emptiness,
just like the Earth here.

Each day, on two planets,
linking light-years of distance,
a soliloquy of sunlight quiets
to a chorus of stars.

A shared strobe of spinning
in residual inertia
from the coalescing of planets –
kindred, never meeting,

parallel as sunbeams.

Orion the Hunter

You are an empty hourglass,
timeless –
slowly cartwheeling the night sky.
Between your legs is a nebula
hanging like a Scottish sporran,
holding seed for the genesis of stars.
You fill a galaxy with your children.

You are a fairy tale –
facing the long horns of the red-eyed bull
to impress the ladies.
Bow drawn, gaze steady,
waiting for your moment.
Waiting.
There is nothing more important than your task.

You are an illusion –
a Rorschach test
revealing the values of others.
Your lights will extinguish
like birthday candles
when Nature makes a wish.

You are just a hollow man
frozen in his agenda –
always seeking, never finding.
You leave it to me to
connect the dots.

The Language of Lines

Wrinkles
from a smile or scrunched nose
write a personality captured over time.
Like an emotional average
or a confession,
lines of age are an epitaph for feelings.

Crescent curves
of worn fingers speak a life
of short natural nails, uneven tone,
and rough skin from hard use in the soil,
long nights of hands wringing alone.

Wrinkles
like furrows worn by stream beds,
overlap like tales written in the dark.
Fragments of lines are experience to be read
like a book broadly open for sharing.

With age,
the smooth page becomes creased
with an alphabet shaped with subtle meaning.
A language gaining voice through new literacy
scattered everywhere on faces for the reading.

Languagelessness

Sensation is a dialect. Your hand
feels warm in mine, pulses transmit in waves as
fervid rivers flow below, seeking confluence
that speaks a new art.

This affinity for you, it is
maternal love desperate admiration lust abandonment fear:
I feel you
as a cloud of want.

I cannot convey the simplest spark
so that you feel it as I do:
all right-brained,
messy and beautiful.

I offer food-chains of emotions,
ecologies of predators feeding on the weak
like an invasive species that eats everything –
brought to the island,
intentions lost, only to find
the insects will rule again.

In my head,
these vague thoughts give me rudder and sail,
while errant sparks in search of words hover nebulously
trying to squeeze their essence into a drop
of liquid life-force.

This nugget I send to you –
If it's abstract enough,
the metaphorical mind might deconvolute it and
you will understand how I feel you,
somewhere between the lines.

Nights of the Waning Half-Moon
(last quarter)

The yin-yang Moon
balanced on Night's fulcrum
a Moon not half empty,
but half full –
like a tree that hides half
to the casual observer,
a wave working pushes with its pull

Reinventing the self
through ebb and deluge –
evolving like the shore,
mutable as the Moon
A slow-strobe dimming
as its vocation,
to one night return
in undulation

Autumn Wane

Trees
release the Sun and wait
for a distant spring.

The garden
fades and I scavenge
to memorize the taste

of summer,
like kissing you
for the last time.

Metronome branches
scrape their strange refrain
as they sway over littered leaves.

Autumn
tells me to cast off withered parts –
things I no longer need. Purge and renew,

and a tree's ring
of wisdom will grow –
there is faith in the fall.

Letting go
gives a hope of new awakening,
like a glimpse of Crescent after New Moon.

And so I open
to autumn to wait for a new season.
What will bloom from this trouble?

Survival
moves through the winter of loss
to find the green of renewal.

Until
it is time
I lie naked as Earth.

It will be mine
in springtime:

Nobody knows
where winter snow goes
except deep roots that feed
to spring forth a weed.

An Only

I've always missed you
in a vague sort of way:
an invented feeling, really,
like missing the ability to fly
or extra limbs.
The truth is
you never existed
except in my longing.

Many times I tried to convince myself
it was better this way, good to be
an only child.
A life without sibling squabbling...

Still, I dream
a half-sibling will surprise me,
appear on my doorstep to
look at me with my own brown eyes
and extend a hand of the same
inexplicably olive skin,
and we would know our timeless bond.
But as decades pass, I know

I am an only.
It seemed worse as a child,
the rainy day boredom...
it was good to hone my imagination
and love of solitude, I said.

Then things became complicated,
and I looked for your knowing glance –
your sympathetic hug –
as we witnessed together the slowly imploding family...
Your absence made me trust myself more, I said.

I offer no aunt or uncle to my children.
There is no shared experience
of the early years
telling me my memories are true.

No one to say: "Yes, I was there too."

Family Photos

Family is sweetness around me, like apple
on my solid core.
Looking at photographs –
slices of days,
captured
and flattened
like
roses.
Family framed in 5-by-7 inch
variegated blooms
in different configurations.
It's impossible to feel the present like this,
objectified and flat.
(memories that weren't memorized
and realities contrived
after the fact)
It's the end of the Five Stages:
Acceptance (tinged
with amorphous longing).
The present
brings a numbness.
It can't be lived before
it's
gone.
We are captive in the echoes
of a revised past.

Family photos
are a carousel.
The bell curve of life spans,
up and down, staggered
birth days,
forced smiles and blurry
candid moments in the whirl.

The topography of a family story.
A little girl wears a pashmina,
looking regal
with train trailing.
She laughs at the wind,
laughs at her brother's funny face.
She laughs freely. She
is
light.
She lives a life without echoes.
A boy wears his grandfather's hat.
They stand in the present.
They are a glimpse
into the future.

Everything is happening
all the time:
emotions and events.
We focus
and click the shutter,
capturing not
the way it was, but the way
we wanted it to be.
An idealized memory, framed
like a poem.

I want to hold tightly
to the people in the photograph,
to the poem
of
family
pressed for future unfolding
like a rare and sleepy rose.
It takes years to see,
how the three-dimensional stands
on the two-dimensional.

The groundwork placed
on the backs of the dancing horses
and the timbre of an echo.
Look yourself in the eyes,
different eyes,
flattened in the photograph,
flattened by acceptance
and jaded by memory.

The path has been cleared,
my bell curve
slopes
downward.
My children walk
behind me. Soon,
it will be their time to lead.
Future generations
will find me flat,
A hollow echo
and a caricature
of
myself.

Cycles of Broken Being
(Sandmirror Oceanglass)

I am sand –
the remnant of seas.
I melt and smooth to glass
to split the sunlight, break the breeze.
A clear liquid sinking,
you can see right through me.

I am glass –
breaking day with the night.
I silver at dusk
and then mimic the light.
A veil between worlds that lifts
the sunrise.

I am mirror –
that breaks to shatter sharply
in slivers of clarity, holding all in my empty.
A vessel waiting
for waves of see.

I am ocean –
breaking stones into dust
I crash mirror-moments,
and comb the memories.
I am cause and effect,
a white noise now gone.

Animal (Human) –
Home (Earth)

Bellows move air through caged balloons
Breathe its gases
Moist undulating soft pipe through
Drink its rivers
Images find the mind in cartwheels
See its mountains
Vibrating cartilage seashells
Hear its oceans

In a leaky package
thermoregulation
Ropes sprout in patches
warmth retention
Private pulses muffled
Nutrient highways
Rubber over scaffold
resist its gravity

We think we are our heads
We think it will be here forever
We sync with its spinning
We sync with its spinning
Our bodies were meant for this place
This place was meant for our bodies
Animal (Human)
Home (Earth)

Life Jewels

The days string together like a necklace.
What do you adorn yourself with?
A garland of laughter.
Love charms.
Trinkets of memories gleaming.
Children like pendants shown proudly.

The clasp is self-made,
held with the strength of years,
survival through storms,
self-actualization
and determination.

If the clasp breaks
everything falls to the floor.
Beads scattered,
disordered,
lost.

Nights of Waning Crescent

A silverfruit eaten by Night
and hollowed by hungry shadow –
the pale light held
abandoned
like the fading of an echo

●

The scoop of a moon
holds this night loosely –
stars dripping through

A sieve that captures
parenthetical questions,
addressed to the Night,
open-ended

●

Sorrow-Moon
bent as an elbow
cradling emptiness

●

How do you hover
held in your place –
skirting the edge
and not flung into space?

Spider

We are more lost than found
and yet always at home
(admit it or not).

Like a spider,
we hold home's creation
within ourselves simply.
Spindled silk, stretched glistening stickily
to points of parameter –
hoping to net the one who will stay.
Storing packages of prey
and waiting for hunger to feed.

Nested in a web of need
I retreat to the language of quiet things –
morning dew and butterfly wing –
the language of the alone.
I build a world, withdraw within
(a project and an oasis)
to dream of green, glorious places
and egg sack bloom
(a day that might not come).

The self remains
(a depth and a destiny)
when all else is empty.

Still Life

I am a snapshot of now,
without the struggle or
the darkness.
Two-dimensional
as a flower in a vase,
I am cut roots, observing
and waiting for rain.
A still life of me
pinned to a scaffold,
a butterfly folded
in silent gaze –
exhibiting the shape but
not the substance.
A mannequin posed
in perpetual curtsey.

Foibles of an Honest Person

…Of extending too far
what cannot be taken back,

Of heartbreak and awkward lurching:
a bear cub bounding with hope.

The desire to live in the undercurrent
than in obscuring waves

Pulling, again and again,
at footfalls dissolved in the wanting.

To strive for the good mirror
that shows life truly,

To be true, a glass
mishandled and chipped,

To live clearly, made porous
like air.

To be a straight tree
with leaves lost and faded,

To be sectioned
and raked into mulch

…or blown away
by dishonest winds.

To be naked
with form intact and obvious.

The Subtlest of Ways

To touch
a stone of rough survival
during days alone and waiting,
while being for the self alone
but not by choice this time.

I fell into the comfortable niche
of me, for I was the one
that could be defined
or unleashed.

It didn't matter
what I took in –
those quiet hours filled
with hollow tendencies – a mirror
world that only I
could see.

But I haven't run
a marathon
of years to lose the win –
yet when there's no one
with whom to build mountains
I fold inward,
a valley, instead.

An origami
torn in the smallest
and subtlest
of ways.

Emergency Department

Wheeled like dim sum
(I make offerings) –

My red rivers spill
in the tapping of the one good vein

While repetitive beeps of wayward machines
rehearse their uninspired 1980s electronica,

And me, writing these words on the back
of an envelope with a borrowed dry erase marker –

(Don't second guess yourself
you did the right thing.)

A night without my children.
I watch them round a distant corner with their father.

"Irregular EKG," the doctor said.
"It's like your heart doesn't know what to do."

"Whose does?" I ask.
Whose does.

Nights of the New Moon

Barren and airless,
holding a light
I cannot see
working worn paths
invisibly...

Faint stars remain
to grant the wishes –
bottom of wane,
Moon fallen to pieces

●

These dark nights without you –
a pull and a promise
of dreams
of reprieve
a moonless faith in silver
or something like gravity

●

Just as shadows
prove the light
this fallow sky
will bloom again

●

Empty Moon –
only the frayed threads
of old suns beam
cold and dead
(a faint light shining in my head)

Death

One day
he popped away
and nobody knew where to

Don't fuss
it will happen to us
and one day will happen to you

Mental Illness

(two poems)

1
Mourning
and letting go of her
would be easier with a funeral
or a physical signal
but

There it is
a disintegrated mind
what other evidence
do I need than
this?

2
She left slowly
so slow
it took half a life
to realize
she was never here

The Life and Death
of a Beloved Victrola

Like a wooden shrine for music
– the Victor Talking Machine of 1904 –
with a cabinet of one-sided albums,
the heirloom of mother and girl.

It sung in braille, crackling and spinning,
as the girl touched its elegant curves.
Just one opera, one time, many years ago –
she sat spellbound at what she had heard.

And then the wild madness moved in…
The victrola sunk battered by squirrels
through winters of neglect and circumstance
yet she kept it for miles and years.

The victrola soon crumbled to pieces
along with the mother, it cracked,
emitting sad songs of silent ghosts
and days that would never come back.

The buckled wood bled an old aria
that no one could hear but the girl.
She stood for a moment, then put it to rest –
and set music free with the birds.

My Heart is Raining

My heart is raining like a cloud –
it drips on dry land, thirst unfilled.
Soaks its stain into the ground;
dark as blood, it paints the field.

Adrift on seas of fallen tears,
I crash to shore rough as a wave,
breaking stones to powdered sand
and cycling back to air unsaved.

My rain is falling, coldness numbs,
wings beating like the migrant geese,
percussion of the circle-drums,
heartbeats bleed delusion's peace.

Grief continues – never ending –
once risen from the darkest seas,
falls again with pressure pending,
knowing that the rain won't cease.

Unspinning the Earth

How would it feel if the Earth stopped moving –
the unperceivable spinning
on this carousel of light –
the Sun like an axle in the center of the Milky Way...
suddenly breaking.

How would we learn to suppress our very breathing
as if frozen in the stillness of day or endless night –
a grieving for the swing and the swirl of normal living,
a halting
and a darkening of everything in sight?

The ceasing of centrifugal leaning from the Sun
would swiftly send us fireward (to burn brightly for a moment) –
digested into everything, then suddenly be gone,
a blip, barely noticed in the churning of the Sun.

To float and be diffuse, to be lost in conflagration,
left with only hope of being one day made anew.

It happens every day
since you went away.

The Fall

How many years
have I watched you, Tree,
turn from bud to cider-red

But this is the last –
for *I* must leave
and won't be coming back again

Collapsing Heart

A heart doesn't break as much as it collapses,
like a dying sun.
A heart falls in on itself, an oblivion
of one.

A heart is a building
that builds itself unskillfully,
digs its cellar clumsily,
then finds itself floating over
nothing in particular.

A collapsing heart is a stopped clock
broken –
it is a moment of the past
that lingers longer than the rest.

A collapsed heart is a memory
kept frozen and fixed
on the one-time for all-time, like a new place
to live.

Yet even now, a future heart
filters the debris,
it gleans what hope remains
and tries coalesce again.

Wishes flung
into the air rain down as shooting stars:
this is the new heart formed in faith –

with the aching of a nebula.

Nights of Waxing Crescent

...in which I ride the scoop of the Moon

The Moon withered wearily
through long nights
ruminating
in old orbits spinning
until she swallowed herself –
and in a peacefulness
of her own making –
birthed herself anew

●

I curl up in your shining curve
a leg hung over the side –
There we hover, you and I
to drift the countryside

●

A slim silvered sigh is all I need
to lie in your lap and survey the skies –
nestled and floating, brisk and alive

●

A slow swoop gliding
I ride
the dark seas –
finding our way
as we sail toward a dream

●

My finger runs along the swoop,
glides smoothly tip to tip –
we fold into
a crescent of crescent
to lie nested, shoulder to hip –
we are two shining spoons
to hold the night –
soon and together
we're finding our light

Axis

It starts with a slant,
a lean on emotion's fulcrum,
a bias to lock in
commitment –

The choice
to be peaceful, happy, and kind
regardless of
external anything.

Happiness is deep,
like an underground spring
to be drawn from at times
like a well.

Still, it takes patience:
the Earth's inclination
will find a spring fine...

as surely to arrive as
sunshine.

Everything

Everything is made
from the remnants of what was

So, yes –
you can build from it, again

The Fear of It

They say that
resistance
to something inevitable
makes it seem worse
than it is. Maybe the trick

is to give in,
try to increase the worry,
bend like a tree in the storm,
give pain its due,
find the center of it and look at it plainly,
turn it carefully
in the palm of your hand,

and realize it can own only so much
of you,
unless you give it more.

It is a balloon
that can get only so big.

Anything more is just the fear of it.

It's Over

It's okay to stop
running, I've come far:
survived,
made it through,
overcame
the night with dawn
and now for me
that time is gone,
a time
boxed and buried,
I'm ready
to shift the weight
forward, take the hard step
and live –
let the flowers wither
with the crumbling stone.

Acceptance

My mother has died. My mother
is alive. She is a reality to be accepted.
She is here but not returning
from her mirror-maze reflections.

Twenty years
of treading and a patchwork
of denial (now cracked and faded)
grants me the unsteady crown.

It is mine alone to wear,
like the loss. No ceremony exists
for this day. It happens in my mind
when I open my eyes.

Actions show a truth
while the mind trails, dragging.
The mind is a weight
to be carried until it finds wings.

Acceptance
is the wind lifting upward to find
the way forward: I am no longer a doing,
I am a becoming.

Matriarch

I've let go
of the illusion that someone else
will lead the way.

No one will take the reins,
no shining light shows the path.
It's time I owned it –
tidied the dark corners,
sat in the dusty throne,
claimed the family heirlooms,
and tossed the dying things.

I will set down the weight of denial
to lift an honest living.

It's time to trust the instinct
that brought me here, today.
The will is strong but uncertain –
(who will teach the children to sew?)

I look to the elephant matriarch
leading her herd. (Does she ever
doubt herself? What does she do
when the lions roar in the night?)
She trusts herself as I do.
I will.

No one stands above me now,
I mold imperfect clay;
I shape the days of family
as I will our way along.

Our path is forged alone,
the labyrinth has straightened
while walking crooked roads –
a new land has awakened.

Inertia of the Past

Some days started years ago.

A ball slipped,
and a moment started rolling
with the inertia of the past –
a force beyond countermanding.

But it's not done yet.
Possessions slip
into successively smaller boxes
until the owner is all that is left,
so the owner is put into a box too:
heart-shaped and vacant.

After generations of climbing
the mountain, all it takes is one
neglectful nudge, one
absent-minded stumble to
careen off a cliff toward the canyon floor,
waiting for the smash and the crumble
in the slow-motion tumble
of bracing years.

The only way to persevere is to refuse to do otherwise.

Greet the canyon floor
arms spread wide and pretend to fly
for just one sparkling second...
Because why not?
Strength is not what is endured by the body,
but what is survived in the heart.

It is the move beyond existing that starts living.

So, find a symbol for the restoration. Heal
in the debris from which to build a new building.
Be the seed that sprouts after the fire.

Release one heartfelt drop of emotion
into the clear pool of the world. Watch
it reach, fingers branching and
diffusing until it is absorbed. Perhaps
a rivulet of hope will reach a heart
that hears better than ears.

And cling to the future like a handhold.
For it is not our shell that keeps us safe
but our core. For the shell is but a
barrier that breaks
when it falls, and the core is
life.

And know the future is a friction —
that holds the promise
of wings.

Hope

Dear Bleeding Heart
overflowing with sadness:

Set despair to dry
in the sunshine.

Make your sadness
as malleable as clay –

A necessary sadness
that builds a new place.

Let it form in the toil
of working hands

That gather what remains –
to bloom again.

Nights of the Waxing Half-Moon (first quarter)

Origami Half-Moon –
she folded her valley
into a mountain

◑

You saved me like a song
sensed but unseen –
I looked for you behind the clouds
and felt you in a billion suns

◑

At last you have returned to me,
the light inside you brimming –
to slip serenely over trees
with place for me in the rising…
Now it's up to us, my True,
our time has now begun anew

A Day Reborn

This day fits in the palm of my hand
like a broken bird grounded from flight –
like the day you left and the day you returned.

Between these is the urge to soar
while staying to be fed:
squat in a cage, numb and content,
with a mind's life already spent.

I sent a wish on the wind
for the new and excruciating
(something like love) –
give me joy so intense I can barely stand it.

So I ran away and ran towards (same thing),
and found home everywhere I looked –
it originated from me like an appetite
that I fed to sweet satisfaction.

I mended clipped wings to stretch a new day to fly.
And all these things expanded to overflowing:
a day of glory uncontainable
and a night un-held, its broad pinions touching the horizons.

That which is closest is hardest to find.
Finding love when all else is given away.
Love loses it all and finds everything.

The Begin

I wonder if endings
are a deception - beginnings
and endings are
intertwined - nothing
truly ceases
to exist - energy endures,
everything
echoes and
continually begins
and begins

Eaten

One idea gestates, then cracks its confines. Hatches.
A second unfolds softly as a bloom.
One hungry day, the form with wings devoured the other.
Being tethered – there was nothing it could do.

The thing with wings ate the dream of green –
they survived as fragrant song, a flourished feathering.
They flew away, a composite of earth and sky,
to live their days together, grounded and soaring.

The Story of the Body

Love your body.
Your body is a story of you, just as
my body is the story of me. The
body is a manifestation of the
uncontrollable things and the flight
you took from them, by your own wing.
The body is a diary of old secrets. It is a
sovereign nation. The body is the things you
accepted and the things you would not accept.
It holds the repository of dreams, and is an
interactive sculpture showing trips around the Sun.
It records seasons of folly, of endurance,
of surrender, of passion. The impact of the mind
on the body, and the impact of the body on the mind.
And the scars left behind are the touchstones
of the stories.

Mothering Anew

Sometimes my children are magical
to me. Sometimes, for a moment,
I forget they are truly mine, that they
gained substance within me. Yet when I
close my eyes in darkened silence, I know
that we are made of the same skin,
and our touch electrifies
in the recognition of mutual belonging.

Sometimes I can barely remember
my children's births. Sometimes I can barely
forget their births and the sickness
that preceded it. Other times
I long to recapture the feeling
of them shifting inside, silently swimming
in their private pond in the moments
before we both were born.

My children are a lifelong dream fulfilled
(they are meant for me). Sometimes
my children make me weary and I wonder
how I will survive. My bones
crumble under the weight
of their need until love arises
like a phoenix to birth mothering anew
(I am meant for them).

Sometimes when I am away from my children
I feel like a teenager roaming
without parents, my mind racing
with pure possibility. Other times, I want to hold
my children forever, and I cup each day
with them in my hands like a precious gem.
I carefully wrap the moments into
memories to open when I am old.

I never feel that I give my children enough
of myself, even when there's nothing left of me
to give. Sometimes I remember
that they have already given me more
than they could ever take. That we
are complementary like breathing.
My children formed me in love to rise out
of the rubble of my old life to be their mother.

New Island

I feel tired.
I am tired.
The woman in the mirror confirms this.
She returns my gaze and asks, "What happened to you?"
Tired and old,

skin sliding from bones
the way snow slides down
a mountainside. Bones grating
together, an overused machine in need of oil.
Snow sliding from a crumbling mountain.

And then
I see my children
running, giggling, frolicking, almost flying.
My sun explodes as I glow from
every pore, awakening
a new dawn. I burst in
giddy gladness and smile so
close to my core that I feel
my soul will break,
its fault lines shifting.

The avalanche stops slipping
from my rocky ridges. My bones
pivot on gleaming new hinges.
I rise and run with my children. I roll
on the floor laughing with them.
I am a volcano forming an
unexpected new island.

Brother and Sister

You began in the same barely-habitable place.
Your hearts beat together with mine
(each one in turn)
in our shared weakened vessel.
I survived through you
as my body practiced its slow betrayal,
just as you survived through me.

You each stuck it out for thirty-seven weeks
then went toward the light, emerging,
long and smooth, to be placed on the outside
of where you were inside.

And then you met.
Like former occupants of the same apartment meeting for tea,
survivors of an uncivil landlord,
you stand parallel, side by side, congruent and bonded,
and now you have the nurture and the nature,
commiseration for parental oddities,
shared holidays, and what to do with Mom someday.
Siblings.

I can only imagine
having a partner for rainy day scheming, fort-building, life.
I will gladly someday leave my life in the hands of this committee of two.

Parenthood

The clouds wrung themselves (like washcloths) –
squeezed their white into gray

Let the overflowing flow (and then some)
until they fell to the ground

Soaking wet
and spent

Living on
in wild flowers

Nights of Waxing Gibbous

Gluttonous Moon
opening wider –
claiming the sky so broad
with her silver

◐

She made a decision
it wasn't enough –
she wanted it all
so she took
another bite
of
sky

A Heart Made of Hearts

A heart is made of hearts,
one from each loved one –
collaged in their keeper (that's me),
an emotional cacophony
dependent as a colony.

What do the hearts do all day?
They pump as a matter of business, thud-ump, thud-ump.
Sometimes they meet for tea
to marvel at their filigree.
But mostly they bleed.

A heart so divided
is always mourning, always rejoicing, always terrified.
The hearts fill my heart like a project:
so bloated, contradicted and panicked,
desperate as an addict.

In this tapestry threaded with textured loss,
the patchwork finds comfort
while scattered loved ones roam,
leaving heart-trails through space-time,
like breadcrumbs to home.

What does the tapestry do?
It filters the flow, netting for a pearl.
It warms like a crowd huddled in diversity,
and eats like a vagrant in scarcity,
anonymous as a city.

I offer you my quilt of threadbare rags,
carefully gathered and colorfully stitched,
fragile in its hoarding like binding sheaves.
An obsessive curator of precious gems, grieving
and groveling to keep away thieves.

But all of this fades when I sail on your breath —
and my grounded heart,
heavy with hearts,
grows wings...
with a harmony that sweetly sings.

House for Sale

There is a story behind every "House For Sale" sign.
The sign stands testament
to drama inside, both quiet and loud, be it –
a desperate packing
or the joyful reaching for boxes.
A move. A family rearrangement. Marriage. Death.

An empty house often brings tears
of one type or another.
The house stands somberly behind the sign,
vulnerable and on display, naked and unfilled.
Waiting.

A house knows when it's empty,
it feels its doors stagnant on their hinges,
the air unmoving except
for the tiny machinations of spiders and squirrels
as Nature reclaims what was once hers.
Dust to dust.

An empty house ages quickly,
cobwebs like nose-hairs grow in breathless doorways.
It rots in its moldy lower extremities,
knee-deep in the ground, immobile,
a victim of circumstance.

An empty house is lost,
feels unloveable except to one
whose heart is true:
one who sees the chiseled structure beneath
the encroachment of neglect,
one who imagines the fullness of family,
a new coat of paint,
the laughter of children as they climb

the tree in the landscaped lawn once overgrown
with weeds.

This is the one who buys the house,
in sickness and in health.
House sold. Sign removed.

My River

My river holds a rock for sitting, moved
by ancient glaciers and rounded
by patient water. My rock is dappled with
olive green moss that covers us as we
sit like stones.

My river is a carrier of things. I set worries
on its surface and watch them float, rafted with the
leaves and the leaving. My river says to keep moving
in the right direction and I'll get there. It waits for me
to fill it as I fill it.

My rain found its home in my river, and
my river bore my rain to relief. Until one
day I stopped the rain draining from
storm-clouds and left-nothing-left but the
Sun shining and the sunshine.

It was the end of crying and days
blurry with salt. I finally became
sick of myself and the sadness. I never thought
I would, as the tears fell without ceasing to
grief-upon-grief.

Time found the end of my river
as my burdens were set down its stream.
The tears that fed it eventually ran dry
on my cheeks, while I was not doing
much of anything.

A Passing Thought

For trees, there isn't a set number of leaves
Hills can be short or quite tall
Lakes can hold any number of fish
So maybe I'm okay, after all

The History of First Meeting

Some people have always been
a part of us, even
before we met.
Like children born into our lives.

Each person vibrates
and collides with the vibrations of others
like interfering waves – constructive or destructive –
histories and reflections,
intangible baggage,
passed like a handshake.

Admittedly, it's a bias, some call it
pheromones
parallel universes
body language
past lives
a sixth sense, or maybe
it's just armor and keys.

Whatever it is,
people stumble when they meet.
Waves collide and the ego (that notorious borrower)
thinks everything is about the self.
You and me,
loving and hating, a watercolor wash, a distorting fog.

Here in the muddle of these wild vibrations I found you.
Hearts uttering their muted words
to be heard as a language unspoken.
Hearts know their own kind.
Maybe the sixth sense is the heart – it says which way to go.

All I know is
we smoothed each other
from the moment we met:
I am a stone in your river and a river for your stone.
We watched the shiny things rust and float away,
to find the patina of years.

Born of colliding waves
that survived the adolescence of egos,
hearts unlocked and smoothed
in the erosion of mutual bleeding –
to find ourselves
carved cleanly like a rose.

You are my not-alone and my together.
We unwrap the minutes as they come, then carry the steady days.
Looking up, there is a nothingness between us and the field of suns.
Nothingness between me and you.
There's nothing in the way.

Love Like Sand

Each grain of sand
is the end of a story:
a stone or spiraled structure
succumbing.

And each grain of sand
is an unending story:
of atoms of stardust uniting
and binding.

Our love is the sand:
a once-careful casting
is dashed in the crashing with
star-numbered others,

revealing that we
are found not in the castles
but in the forever-nuggets,
the everlasting grains.

I will raise a castle of us – anymoon,
anytide (but the ocean always knows where the beach is)...

And so
life will roll in like a wave, a wave,
to level the fortress of us, and yet –
love perseveres in the grains, the grains,
and so we will build us
again, again.

In this
we find the enduring, imperishable,
resilient and malleable,
cohesive as dough that we form in our hands –

And so we will rise,
and rise
again.

Marriage

A tree incorporates the fence –
my finger,
this ring.

I assimilate this shiny thing
like a limb, stretch its muscles, feel
the pull of its striated sinew,
test its impulses.

The ring is me now, the ring is you,
a simple circle rounding
back to us.

What was once a stranger
is now family of family, held
in a circle like gases forming
a new sun.

I wish upon this shape of immense gravity
that holds us, cohesively,
through black velvet nights, newly luminous,
open enough
to make a space for us
in its knowing,
entered like a womb for the growing.

We are two trees surrendered and grafted,
wrapped and wrapping
the ages in rings.

Together, we erect a sculpture
as fanciful and strong
as a child's dream can build. Unencumbered
as a daytime moon.

How

How did you get to be so strong,
they ask
(they always ask)…

But it's barely a choice,
is it?

When shadows move in the forest,
just keep trudging or you'll never get out
(goblins be damned).

How did you get to be so strong –

Well
a life is lived by the one who lives it,
and letting the past
shadow the future
(your future)
is early death –
if you die trying
at least
it's a death on your terms.

So maybe the question is really
how strong
can you become?

Goblins
be damned.

Weather Report

I am
nebulous, my essence
intangible. I drift
aimlessly and offer puddles
with a pressure change.
I am the
wind that messes your hair and chills
your cheek. I invigorate, tousle, dishevel. I rouse
you from slumber.
Energize
me and I become the aurora borealis. I will
take your breath with my
glory.
I am sunshine, pure
radiance, I bask, I bask. I warm my
kingdom. I am the genesis of light.
I am cold tears falling. I am
warm tears falling. I am tears falling
like hard pebbles that dent, a rhythm
of endless rain.
I am bitter cold
Antarctica. Crash into
my iceberg and I will
sink your ship.
I am pure
magnetism. You
will never leave.
I am the troposphere,
of myriad made.
Come closer, brave
ones. Bring your gear.
I am parched and swallowed
in thirst.
I am hot and cold like

porridge.
I am
still and swirling like air.
I am shades of earth
like skin.
I am colorful like dreams,
or a rainbow.

When I

When I was a tree, I hid secrets deeply (dirt
up to my knees) – my roots
entwined with other trees'
like branches twined with leaves.

Then I was the Crescent Moon
and sailed the endless seas. I sank into
a nothingness –
my light was barely seen.

One day I flowered, loosened
my layers, unfolded, reshaped and restructured –
an exotic fruit discovered,
tattered but still beautiful to the bee.

As half
a Moon
I barely knew
which way to go.

So I became a river:
shallow splashing
deep currents churning –
I rounded my way persistently.

Finally
I rose, a Full Moon circling
the brokenness, gathering pieces
to redefine my whole.

And then I realized that
I am the vernal equinox,
surviving dark days, tipping the pivot
toward the LIGHT,

So I think
I will grow a SUNRISE
to let the world know it can start
again.

Wishes Falling

The night I
saw the stars
I wished only
on the first but
then it fell and I
knew they would all
be mine,
one by one,
someday,
I wish I might

Nights of the Second Full Moon

You will survive
more than you expect
earning beauty
in scars of wisdom

○

She embodies love's shape –
a perfect circle – rolling
into itself, only to collapse
again and again,
an elastic thing that stretches
then faithfully returns
as it swirls back
to its curving core

Falling Up

She would lie on the grassy hill –
and imagine
falling up

The feel of the Earth behind her –
as they fell
together

They sailed through constellations –
soaring weightlessly
as one

She led the way fearlessly –
brave
and flying free

Her sadness dissolved like the sky at dusk –
as Joy
filled her with suns

Wayward Wind

Oh, Wayward Wind,
where have you been?
You've traveled over grass.
From trees and leaves,
you swayed and breathed
and crossed the oceans vast.

You blew for years
as your career
from land to endless sky.
Behind you stayed
a life unmade,
left rustled, flat and dry.

You found a town
and settled down
with nothing left to try.
A day spent dressed
in flowers breath
and cloud wisps in the sky.

You nudged a cloud
to other clouds
and rose up to the Sun.
They joined and rained –
the tears of friends!
You're home, you're finally home.

Healing

It's been said before:
deep wounds are slow to heal,
if they heal at all.

But what if we owned the wounds,
the ones that became part of our ecology?
What if we stopped pushing them away,
even the boxed-up ones
that we tried to keep from our food-chains,
and in so doing, found a way to heal
in wholeness?

Maybe we could swim beneath the scars,
clear the dark corners of the mind,
hold close the tender center of our center
like a precious baby,
feel the measured weight of it,
heavy in hand,
and let all of it breathe, finally breathe,
let the air come in and open it up,
and feel the strength of willingly becoming weak.

We could let the hurt rise up slowly,
billowing its mourning like incense rising,
decompress its darkness
like a leaky balloon:
releasing the nothing
that it once held to stretching.

The space that remained
could be a monument to those days –
days that are gone forever.

If we held it close,
we could listen to its sad song,
place flowers at its feet as we wrote it down,
then kill it like an enemy: with love, with love,
a dark sheep finally brought back to the fold.

And then we could dance, dance, dance...
just because we can.

Love Gives the Heart Imagination

They have always been a part of me, I just didn't realize it until I met them.

I thought I knew love, and I did in some way,
but then I gave myself over to it, an instrument in failing health,

twice, completely,
as my children were born like the weaving of a new fabric.

And then I knew –
in stripping layers of self, I had found Love's Basement,

beneath the soil, unnoticed, but giving foundation to all
the stirrings above. Roots that grew my life thereafter.

A love like atmosphere, a shared breath
close and alive, my soul rising in it lighter than air.

A love like a maze in which to be lost is to be found,
a warp of mirrors that shows the true world.

My heart has been stretched by these precious people and their ways.
Now all is pinnacle and base, substance and essence.

Like the baby-thinness of my child's hair. I press sweet curls to my lips
to imprint them, indelibly, into the lines of my mind-book.

Like the exact weight and balance
of my tired child draped across my chest.

Like the dissolution of time
in my child's laughter. Like my children laughing together.

And that's it, isn't it? They are more than two.
Each unto themselves and the monumental force

they are together. Not additive, but multiplicative, exponential, infinite
– boundless as the sky.

Here I am, so desperate and deeply enamored. It's no wonder that
my heart, my emotions, are stretched.

Not as something that would rupture
like a balloon. More the way the imagination gets stretched

with a new fantasy, creating something deeper,
more layered and intricate.

My children have given my heart imagination. Let's call it love.

The Summit

The summit is the hardest
mountain stretch to climb,
not because it's steepest,
but because the bones are tired.

The weary footfalls driven
by borrowed will alone –
the vision of a victory,
the shape of every stone.

It has the best reward:
a view of the valley below,
my own origination,
and every place I've known.

At last I have arrived
the peak at final mile –
a place to set up camp
and stay a little while.

Would I return to the valley
once drank from golden cup?
Perhaps descend to visit
and help someone else up!

Guilt

Something has jostled loose.

I hope
it will not return.

I can feel the familiar shape of it,
it lived there for so long.

The memory of it a dark puzzle piece,
a vacant place still whole.

With time, I hope new things take its place,
perhaps it will fill with birdsong.

It will take time.

The form of it was distinct and had
weight to it.

It will take time
for the springing-back, the filling-in.

I want to be rid of it
and feel
as I do at this moment.

It's gone.

Faith

They say that faith can't be proven,
that faith defies proof yet
there it is
as certain as love itself –
the Big Bang of God's Love
entwined with the fabric of my heart,
threaded with Grace,
as known to me as breath,
and certain as air. A love expanding
for billions of years,
gaining consciousness,
and looking back on itself.
A faith
that embroidered into my life's story
and decorated my heart with hope.

I know faith because I know love,
and I share it, never ending...
embodying the faith
and continuing to expand.

Not Enough is Enough

I've come to accept that
I am not enough
in all the best ways
and that is okay because
I don't have to be –
I know my imperfections
and where I fall short
every day,
so my forgiveness feeds
from the love
of the Most High
who knows my imperfections
and where I fall short
every day,
and tells me:
you are not enough
in all the expected ways
and that is okay because
I Am.

The Language of Beauty

Ignoring beauty must be a learned thing
like not looking at the Sun.

It's a matter of self-preservation
to shield against:

the translucent gems of seashells hewn by waves,

trees built of physics and yearning,

drops of dormant rainbows puddling to a stream,

wisps of white waterfoam tufting in crayon-blue sky,

a planet held invisibly in a deep-raven nothing, speckled
by an audience of suns…

One could go mad with the sensuality of mere living –
eons of wither and bloom, captured in each handful of soil.

I look at the stories. So many stories poring
between my fingers. Each expressing its transient

becoming and being and quiet dissolution,
netted and knotted with others

while time stops in the oneness,
expanding and contracting with each connected breath.

A beauty known only through the experience of it,
intangible as it surpasses all words.

We share this
moment through honest touch,

leave the boat of leaky words on the shore,
its rudder bent, oar splintered by hard paddling.

Here, we acknowledge the limitations of speech,
communicate with fingers a new braille

developed by two as a signaling, as if
each person were standing on a separate island in the bay.

We will come together in this place of inexact awe,
barely breathing

as we soak in the boundless air directly,
bathing in a nameless beauty.

Two Kinds of Happiness

The First
is young wonder
bubbling to a smile –
river surface, casual mirror, shallow stream –
a fairy tale
looking for a shoe made to fit –
a vessel waiting patiently to be filled.
A kite tied and
tethered to any changing weather –
searching outward,
for the elusive,
when the First Happiness
is faced with the mourning wind.

The Second
is slow work
sparked in quiet shadows –
undercurrent, a deep aquifer undammed –
a sky
that has found it is always full of stars –
the beauty in the depth of raw texture.
A canvas
improved after paint is removed –
looking inward
for serenity
as the Second Happiness
sees flower-wishes in a dandelion.

The First surely fails
like a house on weak ground.

The Second is rebirth,
as bright as a sun's epiphany.

The First is the familiar ways we die.
The Second is the new ways we find to live.

Pulling Down the Sun

The moonbreath we see is an illusion
(the Moon is always-full yet mirror-empty)

Unlike the Moon, I *own* the light I shine,
as my fire grows in brightness, spiraling outwardly

So, I pull down the Sun and glow from within
to see possibility in a starfield overarching

There is a constellation of which my light is part –
I sculpt the shape of it, tell its mythology

And I find, like a stone, I am always the perfect size…
I am the stone of my skies

A Note About the Author

Kat Lehmann was born in Pennsylvania and is the only child of an only child: her mother who was later diagnosed with schizophrenia. She became the first person in her family to graduate from college and went on to earn a Ph.D. in biochemistry. She has published in both poetry and science journals. She explores organic forms through her wheel-thrown pottery and has spent months sleeping in a tent while traveling the continental United States. Her poetry and other writings inspire others to persevere through what cannot be changed, find happiness in spite of them, and notice the silent beauty that is everywhere.

Kat lives in Connecticut with her husband, two children, three cats, forty orchids, and the river where she writes, under a clear view of the Moon.

Connect with Kat
Blog www.songsofkat.com
Twitter @songsofkat
Facebook @songsofkat

About the Cover

Each letter 'O' in the title "Moon Full of Moons" depicts a phase of the Moon. The five phases of transformation form darkness into the light—New Moon, Crescent Moon, Half-Moon, Gibbous Moon, and Full Moon—symbolize our journey from dark days into happiness, acceptance, and peacefulness.

The transformation of the Moon is available to us all.

Notes to the Moon

CPSIA information can be obtained at www.ICGtesting.com
Printed in the USA
LVOW11s0823170315

430877LV00003B/74/P